INDEX

Prologue 3

Chapter One: Moving Beyond Religion 4

Chapter Two: God the Great Spirit 16

Chapter Three: The Spiritual Dimension....................19

Chapter Four: Medium vs. Psychic..........................26

Chapter Five: Mental Mediumship...........................29

Chapter Six: Physical Mediumship..........................33

Chapter Seven: Development of Mediumship..............37

Chapter Eight: Trance and Trumpet Séance……………..43

Chapter Nine: Aura and Chakras…………………….52

Chapter Ten: Power of Healing Abilities………………55

Chapter Eleven: God's Laws……………………..61

Chapter Twelve: Decision Time or NDE………………64

Epilogue …………………………………………66

PROLOGUE

As the future unfolds before humankind, it is becoming very self evident that the old mainstream theologians have nothing to offer present day individuals. Those who seek to know the truth look to the Great Spirit to satisfy their quest for a greater understanding of their God.

As humankind emerges into a newfound freedom, it discards the old, out-dated creeds and dogmas that have for so long imprisoned their inner spirits.

Humankind no longer trusts the ancient religious practices that have failed so miserably to bring them out of the current chaos the world is mired in. As the religions of the world continue to give lip service to archaic doctrines, which they inwardly question themselves, humankind now seeks the truths of the spiritual dimension to guide them in today's fast paced world.

Being a spiritual being has nothing to do with religion. God the Great Spirit did not sanction any religion upon the Earth. None whatsoever; God is not Catholic, Hindu, Baptist, Muslim, Protestant, Buddhist, Jewish, or whatever. These and all other religions are creations of humankind, not of the Great Spirit.

Organized religions of the world have killed more innocent people then all the major wars of the twentieth century combined, all in the name of God.

The time has come for humankind to evolve to the next level of its future existence. We must rise up and cast off the chains of bondage that the religions of the world have used to enslave our very souls. Humankind must fulfill its desire for spiritual development, by using our innate abilities to bring us out of the destructive chaos that engulfs our planet today.

Through these abilities humankind shall move forward into the spiritual realm that God the Great Spirit had intended for us, so that we can grow and progress to our fullest potential. The following information will set those who are ready on the correct path to their spiritual evolution in the twenty-first century.

CHAPTER ONE: MOVING BEYOND RELIGION

The time has come for those who are ready to move beyond the religions of the world, those false beliefs that stand in the way of true spiritual progress. Religion has created obstacles and superstitions to confuse and baffle the mindset of the seeking individual. All humankind desire the freedom to seek the eternal truths which God has made available, yet religion has taken dominion over these truths in order to control the weak and ignorant masses of the world.

Humankind need the simple truths of God, while in the human form, to advance their spiritual growth for the time in which they shall return to their true home in the spirit dimension.

Organized religions will attack your right to have the simple truths of God, because once you have them, you will see how useless religion truly is. God wishes you, the ordinary man and woman, to have his truths that are founded upon eternal, natural laws of the spirit. Not some man made laws designed to control your life, and to reinforce their religious power over you. You were given free will in order for you to advance your own spiritual growth; to live your life based on your needs. Not to be lead by those who would use you for their advancement, their personal authority and power. Those who claim to speak for God do not know what God wishes for you. Only you can know where your true path lies as you journey through this life, for you had a hand in choosing what was needed for your spiritual evolution with Gods blessing.

For humankind to be free in mind, body and spirit, we must understand that we require no popes, no priests, no rabbis, no cleric, no temples, no synagogues, and no church of any kind. No system of doctrine or theology need be placed in your path as an obstacle to the simple truths of God the Great Spirit. Unconditional love, from the smallest measure to the highest, love is the key that unlocks our spiritual growth, and it's that simple.

Religion has taught us to judge others, if they do not believe our way or what our holy book says; then they must be damned for all eternity. How can we judge someone else's life, when we know so little of our own?

If you learn no other lesson in life, know this, all material things will simply fade away with time, and the only thing you take with you when you return home to the spirit dimension will be the richness you have contained in your very own nature. Wealth, power and the like will mean nothing to you on the other side. When you have truly found yourself, you will have found the Great Spirit, and then you will know God.

Humankind must oppose the massive complex of falsification imposed upon it by organized religion over the centuries. The time is now upon us to destroy the very foundation of doctrines, which have been superimposed on humankind by those who falsely claim to guide us to God. They not only demand we follow them, they dare claim humankind can only find God through their leadership. God needs no intermediary to speak to his children; he need not seek you out in a mosque, church, synagogue or temple, for you have direct access when the need arises for direct communication, day or night. You just need to utilize your natural abilities, and relearn the proper way to communicate with the spirit dimension. All humankind possess in one degree or another, the ability to make known their thoughts to the Great Spirit. Once you reconnect to the spiritual dimension, you will then be able to receive the thought messages, the answers to your questions that pertain to your personal life that you are living at this very moment.

Once you have been caught up in the effects of organized religion, which is usually imposed at an early age, it is almost impossible for real spiritual truths to penetrate the dense wall of superstition that has been indoctrinated into your very soul. For those who are strong enough to break free, you will no longer be caught up in the selfishness and ignorance of this chaotic world. The knowledge of the spirit dimension will open and you shall realize the greatness that lies within yourself.

As the truth of the Great Spirit grows in the world, it shall predestinate the end of that which separates all peoples. No more class or race distinctions need keep us divided from each other. We shall be as one, and realize we are all the sons and daughters of the Great Spirit and peace shall engulf our planet.

God's message to us is simple, that there are spiritual truths, spiritual knowledge, and spiritual laws that we can access from the spirit dimension and from seeking within ourselves. There we shall find the guidance and help we so desperately pursue in our lives.

The knowledge we gain and the wisdom we learn while in the physical form, are far greater in value to our deathless soul then all the wealth and power we could ever command in our physical world. Poverty and ignorance shall reign all across the Earth until we embrace the spiritual truths of God the Great Spirit, and that requires sacrifice. You cannot build anew without first tearing down that which has been built on falsehoods and deceptions.

Building a strong foundation starts with educating ourselves, and then teaching our children. If you restrain the soul of a child at an early age, you in essence deny them the fundamental rights of freedom; you condemn them to a life of spiritual slavery. Freedom is the essential quality of all education, which leads to true wisdom and spiritual enlightenment. To teach a child to believe in religion's attachment to ancient myths and falsehood's is to infect the child's intellect. A child so influenced, be it intelligent, will reject and discard the erroneous information as it becomes aware of its deception, and shall then turn on those whom it feels misled it at a time when it had no way to resist their deceitful dominion over it. Those less intelligent will be held captive by organized religions power and authority, and they shall force upon their own children a similar fate, which they are unable to break free of themselves.

Children need to be educated in the spiritual truths of God, to live a moral, charitable life, yearning to help those who dwell within their realm of influence, and to be unfailing to the Great Spirit of which they are an essential element. Teach them God's simple law; do unto others as you would have them do unto you. It was given to humankind long before Jesus walked the earth and yet we still fail (or refuse) to understand its simple message.

Too many so-called religions, for too long have they each been with a variation of God's message. That which organized religion holds most precious, in actuality, is of no benefit to humankind. Religion in the past has caused widespread bloodshed, innocents to be tortured, maimed, and burned all in the name of God, yet those ungodly acts did not increase the spirit of humankind by even the smallest measure. Religion has divided humankind into hostile groups, pitting families and nations against each other. As the ancient religions grew in power, so has world disharmony grown; war and upheaval happen on a daily basis in our society of today. How many would murder and destroy today if there were no religious factions inflaming the people to kill in the name of their God? When you take religion out of the equation, humankind has no need to slaughter and violate each other.

It does not matter what an individual calls himself: a Christian, a Hindu, a Muslim, or whatever. That which matters to God is what an individual does with his life. Being of service to others is the spiritual path in life that we should strive for in order to advance our own, personal growth, as we endeavor to be more God-like.

For those who pray, just know that true prayer is a spiritual action, and when it is done correctly, it will provide introspection, so that looking within yourself leads to becoming aware of not only your inner strengths, but of your imperfections as well. This in turn compels you nearer to the Great Spirit, which inspires you to endeavor to reach higher levels of attainment. Simply mouthing holy words in repetition of some symbolic representation achieves nothing. These repetitive imprints attract no one from the spirit dimension, not God, nor do his Angels respond to such, for those prayers create no resonant force, there is no sincerity behind them, and those who speak those prayers do so with indifference. For they have long ceased to contemplate the true meaning of the words they now utter without thinking.

As two examples of prayers which no longer have any potency for their mere act of formality, one being the Muslim's reciting the same prayers five times during the day while facing Mecca, and two would be Christian's uttering the Lord's Prayer each time they hold services. Even when great numbers of people gather together and listen to predetermined words, or speak meaningless prayers; they bring forth no effect upon the physical dimension, or the spiritual dimension. Only when each individual, aware of his inner strength and his inner weakness, is truly inspired to give greater service, then his prayer will manifest itself before the Great Spirit.

True prayer comes forth only when the individual desires to attune itself with the creative force of life. In order for this to take place; the individual must use his spiritual and physical abilities to be of greater service, thus bringing forth his potential gifts, that he may then be an instrument of the infinite energy that gave him the opportunity of physical life.

When your soul desires knowledge, awareness, and depth, that prayer automatically attracts its answer by creating a vibration that brings those who are in tune with your personal vibration. Such as your guardians from the spirit dimension, harmonious family members who have passed over, and those on the other side who are simply attracted by the love emanating from your soul. When you cry out in jeopardy, they tune into your vibration and come forth with help and assistance.

Just be aware; prayer has nothing to do with religion. When you sincerely pray from deep within your very soul, you are simply connecting with the Great Spirit, and the spirit beings he has chosen to watch over your journey here in the physical dimension.

Foolish prayers, such as "Please God, just let me win the Lottery and I'll go to church every Sunday, I swear?" are simply ignored by God and those who are in tune with your vibration. God wants you to grow spiritually, for you are a spiritual being. God cares not for material wealth, or the power it can purchase, he cares about you. Because you and all the others in the physical dimension are a part of him, you are eternal, so prayers that will help you to be of service to others are always met with positive energy and positive action.

Think before you pray, whom are you trying to help? Yourself, for some selfish reason, or God's children, your fellow man, who are in true need?

At this time, let's put forth the real truth concerning the individual known as Jesus, whom the Christians consider to be the Son-of-God. Ancient religion used his lifetime some two thousand years ago to proclaim him to be the 'only' Son-of-God, but these are false claims. This man Jesus was not sent to save humanity, or to die for humankind's sins. The Great Spirit did not invent sin, humankind invented it to use as a tool to enslave the weak and ignorant masses of that time period.

The life that was planned for Jesus was for him to be a teacher and prophet. He would teach by example, and repeat the words of the Great Spirit that had already been given to humankind, yet lost and forgotten throughout the centuries.

Jesus returned to the physical dimension in order to re-teach the abilities humankind had lost over the centuries, and those teachings were meant only for those in that part of the world he lived and taught in. Jesus was a prophet for that time and place, his message was for those individuals living there and his message was not intended for the whole world, especially those of today's society.

Jesus taught by example to show humankind that what he did, all humankind could do if they put forth the same effort. He incarnated to that area because there was no direction with the people, no guidance, and they did not care about themselves. Jesus came to help people understand themselves and to teach them love and respect for each other. He tried to return them back to the simple basics, to bring forth their spiritual side, yet greed and hatred kept the people slaves. The people were too afraid to stand up for themselves, and his words went unheard by the majority.

Almost five hundred years after his death, ancient religious leaders of that later time period seized upon the idea of the Bible, a so-called holy book the church created in order to control and rule over the illiterate and unenlightened masses.

The Bible has undergone many changes since its conception; with over fifty different versions now circulating in our society of today, all of which are incorrect. The basic principles of the Old Testament started out as a history of those known as Jewish. Their history was based not on written, but upon oral traditions throughout the time period the Old Testament professes to cover. Much later it was written down.

Their oral traditions mainly consisted of old Jewish wives' tales filled with wild gossip of events and proceeding's which never actually occurred. Those events that did occur had been exaggerated to the point of being unrecognizable. Basically, the Old Testament was used by organized religion as a fear tactic to repress and keep the ignorant masses in line, and even today, many individuals are afraid of their loving creator due to religions authoritative control over their lives.

As for the New Testament, organized religion chose the life of Jesus to foster into being the son of their fictitious god, the god spoken of in the old testament; a god of death, revenge, and destruction. A god the populace would fear, thus obeying the religious leaders and their rules in order to enslave the common people.

The ancient church then sought out the few known facts concerning the life of Jesus of Nazareth, while adding and subtracting, and fabricating the rest into what is now the new testament of today's bibles. When you take a small amount of truth and combine it with a large amount of falsehood, you come up with the perfect lie, which is never challenged because it contains truth. The multitude submits easily to such fabrication.

Overall, the fictional biblical story of the alleged son-of-god did indeed work to give organized religion basic authority over those who succumbed to their intentional fraud and lies. Some of the more important things Jesus spoke of to the common people, such as, reincarnation as an example, were deleted from the early bible. The religious authority of the time felt it would be easier to regulate the rank and file if they believed in only one lifetime, instead of many.

The greatest problem facing Americans in today's society is the conflict they feel within themselves and they are angry and unhappy spiritually. Few are truly peaceful, or in harmony, the reason being they don't believe in anything anymore, neither in themselves, nor in God the Great Spirit.

You must believe in something, and they don't believe in anything. They have failed themselves and lost their sense of purpose in life. Americans have no strong family bonds anymore, brother kills brother, families scatter. This is one reason children are so insecure, they don't feel the bonding love of family life.

Americans as a majority don't love themselves, therefore, how can they love others. When you don't love yourself, you can't give love, or receive love. Material wealth and power have no place in God's plan for us.

Humankind will one day realize who they truly are in the eyes of the Great Spirit, and that truth shall set them free. Human beings will come to understand that they are spiritual beings from the spirit dimension, living a human experience in this physical dimension we call Earth.

Spirit beings enter this created dimension to learn the lessons of love and truth, or to help others learn those lessons. Through those lessons of love, spirit beings remember their true connection to the Great Spirit, our creator, and begin their journey home in order to reconnect and remember that they are a part of God.

If the bible had been written by God the Great Spirit instead of the unscrupulous clergy of the period, it would have been provided to humankind in the following fashion. As concerning the Old Testament, it would have been written that God had created the spirit beings, which in turn gave companionship to our dear creator. As spiritual beings, when we grow spiritually and expand, so does God the Great Spirit grow and expand.

God in his infinite wisdom provided all spirit beings the ability to create for themselves. Spirits became co-creators in their own right. A group of master teachers, highly advanced spirits, united their abilities under Gods supervision and constructed the dimensional physical world consisting of the universe and the planet we dwell upon, Earth.

Spirit beings then entered into that created dimension by mentally projecting themselves into the material aspects they found there. They fabricated all animate and inanimate forms in order to experience that which they were now creating at will. Over a long period of time, these spirit beings became trapped inside their own creations, losing their awareness of who they were and of who their Creator was. At that point many were trapped in the living mineral and lower animal life forms of the primitive planet earth, which was still evolving as the universe was in its infancy.

God then allowed another group of spirit beings to enter this created dimension in order to bring forth the human form, in order to help those trapped to free themselves and return to their loving creator. This was based on the human form using cycles of incarnations.

Those spirits that entered the new physical dimension begun to create at will, and gave birth to odd monstrosities of their own making, such creatures as centaurs, mermaids, and unicorns to name a few. Introducing the human form allowed the trapped spirits the ability to project themselves into the newly developed human forms. Through the human incarnations they could free themselves of the animal-mineral forms and return to the awareness of 'who' they were and of 'who' their loving Creator was.

The length of time and the number of incarnations required to restore and free a trapped spirit being depended mainly upon how disfigured it was, physically, mentally, and/or emotionally.

As for the New Testament, had God written the story of 'Jesus of Nazareth' it would have simply told of a mortal man who came to a region of the Earth that was in disparate need of guidance. Jesus was a teacher and prophet who came to help the people break free of their 'self imposed' bondage.

Here is the true version of the life of the man known as 'Jesus' that organized religion does not want you to be made aware of, for the truth would remove all doubt from your mind as to their right to have continued authority over your present life.

Jesus was not born in Bethlehem, because his parents were members of the Order of Essences. Essences were looked down upon and even tormented, and at times even murdered by the Romans. To avoid trouble Joseph and Mary took up lodging with a small group of Nomads several miles outside the city.

Joseph was not the biological father of Jesus, nor did Mary become pregnant by God or by any miraculous or immaculate act on the part of God. That was just an untruth told by the Clergy in order to show Jesus as the Son of God. Jesus came to be a teacher, not a savior for humankind.

Mary had been the victim of rape and impregnated by a young barbaric Roman soldier, the shame and fear of being cast out, or even murdered, kept her from speaking of the incident.

The story of three wise men following a star to Bethlehem was total fabrication on the part of organized religion, just a tall tale to bolster the story of his so-called immaculate birth, in order to show his divine connection with God.

The miracles spoken of in the bible were not miracles at all, most were falsehoods made up by ancient religion. Jesus simply mastered the ability of communicating from the physical dimension with those in the spiritual dimension. From his early instruction to his advanced teachings in Egypt he mastered levitation, astrology, healing and numerology among other things. He received many tests and initiations in the great pyramid of Egypt in order to advance his knowledge and abilities to further help the people of that time and place. Jesus used no miracles to help his fellow man, all individuals have the same potential, the same natural abilities that Jesus used to heal the blind, enable the lame to walk, restore the sick and diseased to health and vigor again. If humankind truly applied their selves to the God-energy, all could do as Jesus did. There were no miracles, all simply according to God's natural laws in the physical dimension. When Jesus walked upon water, it was simply his spirit helpers who levitated his physical body over the water, which gave the appearance from a distance that he was walking upon the water. Not a miracle, simply one of many gifts humankind has lost over the centuries.

Through dreams, Mary was made aware that her son Jesus would become a teacher of men and when the time came for him to go forth to study and learn in other lands, she was supportive in her frame of mind.

Concerning the ruler Herod, he was told by his counsel that a threat to his position existed as foretold by the prophecy which had been circulated long before the birth of Jesus, and that the man who would be King of the Jews had been born recently. The name Jesus was not mentioned to Herod, only that a threat to his rule existed. Thus he acted out of great fear and superstition when he ordered the deaths of all male children up to the age of two. Many children escaped the death decree through various means of ruse and deception. Some of Herod's own men defied his orders and refused to murder infants.

Jesus of Nazareth spoke Aramaic, and could read Hebrew. He later picked up basic Greek and Latin during his studies and travels, and no he never heard or spoke English during that lifetime.

During his middle and late twenties, his physical appearance was that of a dark complexion, and a stout muscular build, with short hair and no beard or mustache. His weight was on average one hundred and eighty-eight pounds and he stood five feet ten inches. His true appearance in no way, shape or form resembled the pale, thin, sickly man with long hair, beard and mustache, which adorns today's crucifix and pictures hanging in churches and private homes.

Be it known that John the Baptist and Jesus of Nazareth knew of each other but no meeting between the two ever took place, for they differed greatly on their ideologies. Ancient religion made up the fictional account of the baptism of Jesus by John the Baptist to accommodate their needs.

The Last Supper never took place and there were no twelve poor disciples. Jesus did have a following of devoted individuals who traveled with him through the small towns and villages, but they were not poor. By today's standards several of his trusted companions would have been considered wealthy, and money was not a concern. The Church had fostered the notion to the masses that Jesus and his followers were poor in order to invoke the sympathies of the common folk so they would feel that he was one of them and not of the richer class. Just note, Jesus was not rich in the way of wealth, but rich in the way of the Spirit.

When it was said he spoke in parables, at first this was not true, yet midway through he turned to using parables in order to reach those who were uneducated who simply couldn't understand his teachings. The short stories were well received and could easily be remembered. Just know those words were spoken for those individuals living during his lifetime, in that particular area of the world. They were not meant for today's society or in this part of the world. We are living in different times and the meaning of his words no longer hold true for the nations and peoples living in the present.

Concerning the Ten Commandments, these were ancient religion's attempt at further control. God the Great Spirit never gave humankind such commandments to live by that would contradict his gift of free will while in the physical form. Once spiritual awareness is achieved in the physical dimension; the lessons of war, rape, starvation, disease and the like will be understood and humankind will embrace those life experiences.

The Jewish leaders of the time feared Jesus would start a rebellion against the Romans and against their rule as well. Even though Jesus was simply teaching a return to brotherly love and showing how to heal the sick, there were those known as Zealots who came to hear his message. Zealots were those who openly fought the Roman rule therefore the Roman and Jewish leaders considered Jesus to be a rebel. Since Jesus did not agree with how the Jewish authority conducted itself before the people Jesus made statements denouncing them at some of his gatherings. This brought about the fear that invoked the Jewish leaders to seek the arrest of Jesus in order to keep their limited authority under the Romans dominion over them. The Jewish vanguard finally persuaded the Romans to arrest Jesus by stating he refused to pay tribute to Rome and tried to prevent his followers from paying as well. This was still not enough for the Romans, who did not want to be involved in what they considered to be a local matter. So the Jewish adjudicator falsely stated Jesus claimed to be the 'King of the Jews' at which point he was arrested and given a mock judgement by the local Roman administrator who in order to appease the Jews ordered Jesus to a mock crucifixion. After being crucified and left on the 'T' shaped cross for several hours (no spikes or nails were used on his hands or feet, just rope cords) he was taken down and ordered to leave the city.

Pontius Pilate the Roman governor had been made aware of what was taking place but he never personally seen or spoke to Jesus of Nazareth. The Romans already had their hands full in this province dealing with the Zealots and didn't need to add this controversy to their list of problems.

The bible story of the crucifixion of Jesus was just another attempt of organized religion to show Jesus to be divine, simply more story telling on their part. Jesus of Nazareth married and did not leave the physical dimension until his eighty-first birthday; he came to teach, not pretend to be the Son of God and lead others into falsehood.

There are those in the physical form who have been taught to believe in Heaven and Hell, actually those two places do not exist, only in the minds of humankind do they dwell. Lucifer the so-called angel or devil never really existed as an individual, he was not a fallen angel, it was just another story the clergy concocted in order to show the difference between good and evil, right and wrong. Obey our rules or you will be treated badly according to the church.

Those who might ask if there is no Heaven or Hell where do we go? When your physical body dies, your spirit leaves the physical dimension and returns to the spirit dimension from which you originally came. There in the spiritual dimension you will take on an ethereal body, which is similar in appearance to your last earthly form. Once you have completed all your physical incarnations and have returned to the spiritual dimension, you then strive to progress to the True dimension, where you would have no need of a shape or form.

When you incarnate into the physical dimension, or as some say, when you are born on Earth, it is required that one forgets the spirit dimension. This is required so the individual keeps from being overwhelmed with past information of other lives, or other sojourns you have experienced in other dimensional areas.

For those who ask where they go after leaving their physical body let me give you one example. In the physical dimension that which is called Earth, everyone lives on the same level. Right now, in the country you are living in, there are people who are geniuses, and there are people who are complete morons and many in between. All are living on the same level. In the spirit dimension, there is a separation. The spirit world contains seven main levels and each main level contains seven sub-levels.

Basically the third main level is where the average, normal spirit would go upon leaving your dimension through the avenue called death. As an example, if you are in the physical dimension, you grow old and pass away. Say you lived an average life, your spirit would then return to the third main level, sub-level number five in the spirit world. There are seven sub-levels in the third main level and you went to the fifth sub-level of the third main level. That is what your life on Earth brought you.

Now you are on the third main level, sub-level five in the spirit dimension in an ethereal body. After dwelling there for awhile, you show interest in rising above that situation. For example, say you grew through knowledge, teachings and incarnations to where you raised your vibrations so you could qualify to advance. At that point, you would be ready to evolve to the sixth sub-level of the third main level. When you desire and achieve success there, you could move right into the seventh sub-level of the third main level. When you master all on the seventh sub-level of the third main level you then go to the fourth main level, but you would start out on the first sub-level of the fourth main level. You would have to go through those seven sub-levels before you graduated to the fifth main level.

A person in the physical dimension, who was a loving, spiritual and helpful person to his fellow human beings while on Earth could easily pass over and go to a higher level in the spiritual dimension. Out of the seven main levels, anything below the third main level is not desired. You want to progress out of the first and second main levels as quickly as possible. You would not want to associate with those low spirit beings. Yet, there are spirits who enjoy being there, where they fight, steal, and connive. Those who murdered, raped and the like who did not learn the spirit lesson behind those acts they committed, but enjoyed the animalistic chaos they brought forth return to the lower two main levels.

Spirits on the sub-level above you are always encouraging you to improve and progress up to where they are. You would be doing the same for those spirits who are on the sub-level below you. God the Great Spirit leaves no one behind, there are no lost souls.

In the spirit dimension there are seven main levels and each contains seven sub-levels. God's idea is that we each continue to evolve so that when we reach the seventh sub-level of the seventh main level we will be ready to enter then into the True dimension, the one in which we could never, ever again be returned to a physical form. When you have mastered the seventh sub-level of the seventh main level, you enter the next blueprint, the next concept God has planned for us. At that time you release the ethereal body, or what some refer to as the soul body, for that is no longer required as you become pure spirit. At that phase you begin again at the bottom, but you are now pure spirit, dwelling in the True dimension. Gods plan is a never ending experience, for we never achieve completeness, because, there will always be more to learn and experience. Basically, God the Great Spirit starts us up, and then lets his creations, the higher evolved spirits take over and run things, for as we grow and expand, God grows and expands.

Remember the Creator is within each individual, not in some false holy book. Just know you are living in this created physical dimension on the planet Earth. This very time period is the most morally delinquent and unethical in the entire evolution of our world to date, and we are living right in the middle of it. Humankind has lost faith in God, their leaders, and in them selves.

If you were able to compare your past lives you have already lived on the Earth, to this present life you are currently living now, you too would agree it is by far the filthiest existence you have ever encountered. This is due to all of the intellectual slop and garbage being thrown at humankind through books, television, newspapers, radio and the Internet. Humankind is bombarded day and night with these influences of treachery, fraud, and deceit. This is the worst era of the physical dimension to date, and it is not improving as time passes. The time has truly come for us to evolve higher spiritually.

Seek within to find the true wisdom of our loving Great Spirit. Share the wisdom of God freely with all that seek it. Don't sell it or force it upon others who don't care for the knowledge, many have not yet evolved through their incarnations to where they can understand the wisdom, but those who have evolved high enough to understand it, give it freely.

A HUNDRED YEAR PERIOD TO HUMANKIND IS BUT A MERE BLINK OF AN EYE TO THOSE IN THE SPIRITUAL DIMENSION, FOR TIME AND SPACE LIVE ONLY IN THE MIND OF THOSE IN THE PHYSICAL DIMENSION.

CHAPTER TWO: GOD THE GREAT SPIRIT

Many ask, "Who or what is God?" God is the supreme universal energy, the eternal creator of all things animate and inanimate. God is the whole vastness of life. God is not an individual. God the Great Spirit is all perfection, a force, an achievement.

It would be like saying; I want my diploma, so I will go through all of these challenges of schooling and studying to reach that goal. God is the goal that you are reaching for in perfection of life, of that which is beautiful, pleasant and desired.

The Great Spirit is all energy, all life, all beauty and all accomplishments completed. That is God in a nutshell.

Now through this wisdom, intelligence and perfection, God-like men and women do those works which draw attention to God, to that supreme energy, to that supreme conclusion of life. Those works: being of service to humankind in the way of healing the sick and infirm, comforting the mourner, guiding the bewildered, giving strength to the fatigued and direction to those who have lost their way. For humankind there is no higher service then these accomplishments in the eyes of God. Do not seek recognition or praise; just know you are fulfilling the true purpose for which you entered into this world, to bring enlightenment to yourself and to those who need your help.

Remember, when you die and leave the physical dimension and return to the spirit dimension that is not the end of life. You won't be sitting on a fluffy white cloud playing a harp for the rest of eternity; you will be seeking to evolve higher, to achieve being more God-like in your own spiritual development. To be absorbed through this supreme energy called God, in order for everything to be in harmony, in correctness and that everything will have the proper answer.

Do not fear being absorbed, for you still retain your individuality. You are simply adding your energy to that of Gods energy. God continues to expand, like adding wood to a fire, the more logs you throw on, the larger the fire becomes. The more spirit beings that become God-like, the stronger Gods energy becomes. You become a part of that energy, to where that intelligence can reach out and touch other spirits, thus making this a more integral truism of the universe, more in exactness, more in balance. Whereby the fundamental control of human life and death in the physical body—weather conditions, drought and starvation—will be in preciseness rather than all the turmoil it is in today.

The Earthly ideals of assessment of oneself have nothing to do with Gods evaluation of us. That which our world worships and craves such as position, power, wealth and authority is inconsequential to God the Great Spirit. The service we have rendered to our fellow beings out of true love and affection all aid to increase our spiritual character, which helps attain our goal of becoming more God-like. That is what God seeks from us.

Many have wondered when life truly begins in the womb of the average female in the physical dimension. True life does not take place until the spirit enters the physical body of the baby. The normal entry of the spirit entity—there are some exceptions—takes place just seconds before the actual birth of the baby.

During the basic nine-month period when the baby's physical body is growing inside the mother's womb, it is merely an extension of the mother's body. The baby has no existence of its own until the actual time of birth when the spirit enters and occupies the physical body of the baby. The baby is merely an empty shell until the spirit moves in to give it life.

Keep in mind that the spirit entity is still receiving last minute instructions prior to its incarnation, its birth into the physical dimension.

Let us reiterate once more on the controversial subject of abortion. When a physician performs an abortion he/she is simply removing an empty shell that has no life force. While the small body is inside the womb it is simply an extension of the mother's body, sustained only by the umbilical cord.

At no point in time is the mother violating the laws of God by undergoing an abortion, and at no point in time is the physician violating the laws of God by performing an abortion. God's laws have nothing to do with humankind's laws. God's laws are eternal, they remain constant and do not change, whereas, humankind's laws are ever changing, one day for, the next against.

OUR PHYSICAL BODIES ARE CREATED WITH BILLIONS OF CELLS AND EACH IS A LIVING ORGANISM.

GOD IS MADE UP OF INFINITE SPIRIT BEINGS AND EACH IS AN INDIVIDUAL ENTITY.

AS A METAPHOR IT CAN BE SAID THE GREAT SPIRIT IS THE BODY AND WE ARE THE CELLS.

CHAPTER THREE: THE SPIRITUAL DIMENSION

It could be said of the spirit dimension that it fills the boundless amplitude of space as rationalized by humankind. The earth is encircled by the seven main levels and their corresponding seven sub-levels just as all the planets contain their own individual spirit dimensions which are higher or lower in their rarefied oscillation levels. All these spirit dimensions meet and blend together, so when you master one spiritual dimension you are then prepared to enter into another spirit dimension on another planetary level if you so desire. For a better understanding, just think of these dimensions as being a state of consciousness rather than a physical place.

In the physical dimension humankind on Earth utilize their senses which in turn make all physical objects seem real to them. This is the same for those in the spiritual dimension where their spirit body is functioning on a higher vibrational level. That which is beyond our senses is real to those who are not held down by Earth's denseness in a higher vibrating dimension. Beauty in higher dimensions is almost impossible to compare or imagine for those dwelling in the created low vibrational dimension of earth.

In the spirit dimension sounds, colors, and even fragrant smells can make up a spirit beings name, or combination of names. There are highly developed spirit entities that are seen simply as multicolored rainbows because of how much they have progressed through the higher levels of the spirit dimension.

There are those in the spirit dimension which can lower their vibrations to where they can penetrate into our physical dimension. Everything in our world, including us, give the appearance of a shadow or reflection to them, to where they can perceive us, yet nothing impedes their movement as they pass through our dimension. There are also those who can walk among us for a limited time and appear physical and real to our senses.

Communication in the spirit dimension is accomplished by spirit beings sending and receiving pure thoughts. Thoughts in their pure form are not misunderstood. They convey the exact intended message as it was meant to be. Unlike the spoken word in our physical dimension which is commonly misunderstood in its meaning and content and therefore causes all kinds of problems and confusion.

The cycle of incarnations, or reincarnation as some call it is merely the process chosen by many spirit beings as a way to advance or progress at a faster rate. One can progress just the same in the spiritual dimension without ever incarnating into a physical body in a physical dimension, yet advancement can be accomplished at an accelerated rate by incarnating. It is up to the spiritual individual as to which path they choose.

Speaking of cycles, just know there are many different types of cycles connected to the Earth. Spiritual, mental, emotional and physical cycles; each individual is capable of experiencing these in the physical dimension. These experiences for the majority of humans are the same experiences that humankind has been facing for centuries. Yet, you now live in a different era of time, a different environment of advancement of humankind itself. The experience is still relatively the same basic experience you came to learn; how to get along with your fellow human beings, how to survive, and how to help one another or how not too.

Therefore, basic experiences run in cycles. An example would be that of a Caveman challenging another Caveman, fighting over an injured animal, both feels it is their property and that they have a right to it. That same learning cycle is in effect right now in your society of today. People are challenging each other over who owns what. You still have your disputes over whose property or territory is whose.

Now, your life itself many times can run in cycles. Be conscious of the knowledge that you can control these basic cycles in your life, the highs and lows. Some individuals have just one complete cycle while others may have many. A person in control of his life can control their cycles, whether they are aware of it or not.

There are many different cycles occurring on many levels at the same time in your life. Growth cycles, learning cycles, astrological cycles, Earth cycles and so on. Now, if you know and realize that you are in a particular cycle, fine. But remember never wait for a cycle to do something or wait for a particular effect to take place. If you allow a cycle to control you, you lose your free will.

An example would be if you are one who follows the astrological forecasts or what some call horoscopes, do not make personal decisions based on what is printed in those books, magazines or newspapers, nor what is put on the Internet. Do not allow yourself to be controlled by the Sun, Moon and Planets in your dimension. Break those controlling influences by using your God given free will.

If you wish to read such information, do so for amusement only. Then go out and live your life to its fullest degree, seek truth from within and follow your true path in life chosen by you. And just know sitting in front of the television or computer day after day is not a good path to follow in life.

The Akashic Records contain the infinite wisdom and knowledge of God the Great Spirit, and since we are co-creators with God we have access to these collective thoughts that span eternity when in the spiritual dimension.

Part of this includes our life blueprint, which we chose before we enter into a physical body, those things we wish to achieve or overcome in a particular lifetime. Such as when we will be born and who the ideal parents might be to best help us with the lessons we chose to deal with. The parent(s) might be the lesson itself. We are allowed to choose all major events that come into our lives, such events teach the most powerful and life changing lessons to us. For instance, one may develop a crippling illness whether it is you who require it, or that of a friend; to teach us the power of love and compassion on an individual level.

The lesson of rape can be experienced on either the level of victim or the level of assailant. It may be hard to understand on a physical level the lesson of rape, yet on a spiritual level the rapist and the victim may in fact be a close friend in the spiritual dimension. They both agree on the spirit side who will be the attacker and who will be the intended victim in order to experience a negative event in the physical dimension, which cannot be experienced in the spirit dimension. In another incarnation these two close spirit beings reincarnate and switch roles, the attacker is now the victim and the victim is now the attacker in order to fulfill their desires to experience such an event that is unattainable on the spirit side. Seeing the love behind such an event is extremely hard while in the physical form yet becomes crystal clear when you return to the spiritual dimension and see it as a life lesson.

All major life events that happen are basically programmed into our blueprints by us to further our spiritual development. These blueprints are placed in our subconscious mind to help us fulfill our individual pattern of growth. Just remember this, we do have free will to alter and change our blueprint once we incarnate into the physical world. We may do even better then we ourselves foresaw or we may not only take the wrong path in life, we may lose ground due to our misuse of our free will. This is where your Guardian Angel plays a role in your life, trying to help and guide you on your chosen path.

During our time on Earth, there is basic testing going on to see how we are going to react. Certain events that happen to us are simply a test period for each individual. For example, when there is a big layoff at a plant or factory, three hundred workers are laid off. Three hundred individuals are being tested to see how they are going to react. Are they going to give up and go get drunk, go steal or will they go find another job? Then later when they pass over to the spirit dimension, and end up on the first sub-level of the third main level, it will be explained to them why they are on a lower sub-level then others they knew. Because when everyone else was laid off, they went out and found new employment, you on the other hand got drunk and gave up. That is why you are here and they are on a higher sub-level.

You are simply being tested; this is a crisis in your life. Your guardian angel will be watching to see how you handle the crisis, to see what you are made of, your character. God is interested in building character. No matter how low an experience in life may seem; that may be the very experience that snaps an individual into a very high level or sub-level in the spirit dimension based on how they handled it and what action they take based on the crisis.

You may be asked when you pass over, "What did you say to the dummy you saw walking around on the street?" You might have said, "Get out of my way. You make me sick. I can't stand to look at you with slobber and snot on your dirty face." What is the first question your guardian angel will ask you? "How did you treat that dummy?" You will reply, "He made me sick, I had to run him off." Then your angel will show you the 'Archangel' that the dummy was. It is all testing. Not testing to be cruel to you, it is testing to improve you, to improve your spirit. To help you love and understand your fellow man, who is simply another of Gods creations. We are all a part of each other and of God the Great Spirit.

When all is said and done in your life, this life you are living now, and you die and cross over to the spirit dimension, you are given the wonderful opportunity to judge that lifetime you just left. No one judges that life except you, not God, not your guardian angel, no one but you. You are given a Life Review in which to refresh your memory of that life you just finished; it comes forth in a detailed chronological progression.

When you judge your life you feel no pressure from others, you do so for your own benefit to see where you achieved and where you regressed in your original blueprint. Now there are those upon return who simply cannot face their life review and own up to the horrible way they treated themselves and/or treated others while on Earth. Those individuals are then counseled by higher spiritual beings that go over their life review with them to bring them to an understanding of where they erred and went astray of the life they had planned. In those instances it may take a long time to bring the spirit being to the point where they can face up to what they have done in the human form. At no time are they forced or punished, just made aware why they are on such a very low main level, such as main level one or two, and what needs to be done to improve their self imposed situation.

An example would be the life of the one known as Adolf Hitler. He returned to the fourth sub-level of the first main level of the spirit dimension. That spirit which lived that incarnation is undergoing many hard classes seeking to improve and overcome the weakness that led it to such destruction while in the physical dimension. Just know those spirit beings who gave their lives in the Holocaust did so freely in order to teach the world a most important lesson. Individual growth knows no limits, it can teach one individual or it can teach many.

God the Great Spirit does not judge you for what you yourself chose. People on Earth say things like, "How could God do this to me?" or "Why has God allowed this evil thing to happen?" God did not do anything to you or them except grant your request to live in a physical body of your own choosing. All major events that happen in your individual lifetime are for your growth and experience, of which you yourself chose to occur.

Now let's turn to those who dwell in the spiritual dimension and assist those in the physical dimension. Let us first deal with those individuals who are seeking to acquire some type of spiritual development or what may be termed some type of mediumistic development while in the physical dimension. Once they start in earnest on this path they will summon to them what would be called an inner band. This inner band would consist mainly of a Master Teacher, a Guardian Angel, a Chemist, an Indian Chief, a Doorkeeper or Messenger Guide, a Health Guide and sometimes a helper of the White Sisterhood Order.

The Master Teacher is far higher spiritually, far removed from the physical dimension in highness and awareness. They are an exceptionally elevated spiritual being, even vastly more so then the Guardian Angel. The Master Teacher observes and watches what the others in your inner band are doing in regards to that life you are living in the physical world. He has to approve what your Guardian Angel and the other helpers to you are doing. He makes the final decision in your life. When you reach the point of death, he and he alone is the one who decides if your spirit can leave the physical body and return to the spirit dimension or stay in the body and finish out your blueprint. If it is time to return he will send your Guardian Angel to bring you home. If it is not time for you to die, your Guardian Angel will instruct your spirit to remain in the physical body. Your Master Teacher is not usually in tune with you on a constant basis, yet he is situated where if he were needed your other inner band members could contact him should the need arise. If some dire unforeseen event should present itself and your Guardian Angel was unable to handle it the Master Teacher would be notified immediately should it concern your death.

The Guardian Angel is the main teacher and supervisor over the works of the other guides who come to work and assist you. He okay's what the others do for you.

Your Chemist is responsible for manipulating the intellect and chemical actions necessary to produce whatever is needed from your physical body depending on what type of mediumistic development you are attempting to unfold.

The Indian Chief usually but not necessarily refers to Native American Indians. Sometimes depending on what type of development is sought more than one Indian join's your inner band. He mainly plays a large part in producing the energy needed for healing and physical phenomena and also provides protection for his medium while in a Trance State as well as in his daily life.

The Doorkeeper or Messenger Guide usually comes in the form of a child, sometimes as an Indian boy or girl. This guide's main duty for those seeking development is to act as a telephone operator or doorkeeper in allowing other spirit beings who are not part of your inner band to use you and your abilities to communicate with those on Earth. It is their job to see that, if they so allow, others do not misuse or cause harm to you in any way. Low spirit beings are never allowed near you while communication is taking place between the spiritual dimension and that of the physical dimension.

For those who are not seeking spiritual development this guide simply assists in the way of helping us in such areas concerning physical healing or in emergency type situations. If they cannot help, they are in a position to contact those who can. Should you require help due to illness or some dire problem presents itself, you can seek help from your spirit guide for their assistance. Send your thought mentally to them. In a short while you'll be surprised at the thought answer that pops into your head.

The Health Guide mainly comes to advise you on what is needed to help your development in the way of nutrition and/or exercise for your physical body.

Sometimes a guide from the White Sisterhood, an organization in the spirit dimension which like minded spirits have joined together to do good works, will join your inner band.

For most individuals on Earth who are not seeking some type of spiritual development they have an inner band consisting of a Guardian Angel and a Messenger Guide, who watch over and assist as necessary or when called upon to do so. A Master Teacher usually does not have contact until that lifetime is nearly completed, then they decide if it is time or not to return home.

There are times during your life that you will hear people speak about the 'Higher Self.' No one can reach their Higher Self until they lose their physical body in the physical dimension and they lose their spiritual or ethereal body in the spiritual dimension. You cannot reach it through yoga, meditation, DVD tapes, books, or seeking inward. Those who say you can are just trying to sell their books or tapes or whatever to make money.

When you progress to the seventh sub-level of the seventh main level and you are now crossing over into the True dimension—where no shape or form or body is necessary—you are now pure spirit or that which you would call your Higher Self.

HUMANKIND WILL ONE DAY UNDERSTAND WHAT THEIR LOVING GOD HAS ALLOWED THEM TO EXPERIENCE IN THE WAY OF WAR, RAPE, DISEASE, STARVATION, MURDER AND THE LIKE…AND THEY SHALL BE SO VERY THANKFUL FOR THOSE LESSONS.

CHAPTER FOUR: MEDIUM vs. PSYCHIC

At this point let's explain the differences between a Medium and a Psychic. A psychic person is one who is limited in what they can pick up from their extra-sensory perception or what is commonly called ESP. Using their ESP they are at no time in tune with or connected to the spiritual dimension or to anyone living in the spiritual dimension.

The main problem with psychics is that they register the vibrations emanating from the individual who has engaged them for a reading. As an example, say you just came from your Doctors office and an X-ray showed a spot on your lung and your Doctor wants you to return to run more tests to determine the cause of the spot. In the mean time you start worrying that you may have lung cancer. You now decide to go to a psychic and see what they say. The psychic picks up the thought vibrations you yourself are putting out over your fear that you might have cancer and then the psychic says they are picking up cancer and ask if you have seen a Doctor? You then are convinced you have a cancer by the confirmation of the psychic's comments, yet you may not in fact have a cancer because the psychic is simply reading your own vibrations of fear and doubt. Your later visits to your Doctor may prove the spot to be nothing of a serious nature.

Now a psychic can be of limited help in the way of picking up some thought vibrations emanating from you that deal with your sub-conscious. They may hit on something your sub-conscious is dealing with that you are not consciously aware of at the moment. This could possibly give you an opportunity to start thinking consciously about the concern.

Be very leery of those who call themselves phone psychic's for they cannot read your vibrations over the phone, the majority simply have some type of counseling ability and are trying to keep you on the phone as long as possible to make money.

Mediums on the other hand, unlike Psychics are in tune with those in the spiritual dimension. The job of the medium is to act as a link between you and those in the spirit dimension. Using their abilities in clairvoyance (seeing) and clairaudience (hearing) they relay your questions or concerns to those on the other side and then provide you with their responses. That is their basic function. Be weary of any medium who asks for large sums of money and the like, many fakes and charlatans abound in our sinister world of today.

A Trance Medium is one that is more developed in such a way to allow their guardian angel or another in their inner band to use them physically. They can lower their vibrational level to where they can speak directly to you without the interference of the medium's mental or emotional sensibilities interfering with their direct communication. If you can find a true Trance Medium then that is the one to engage for a reading with the most accuracy, unfortunately, they are becoming a rare breed in the physical dimension. Most mediums don't or won't put in the necessary time to develop this wonderful gift.

When they are taken into a state of deep trance, their spirit will step aside mentally in order for their inner band member to step in and control mentally their physical body to bring forth the desired phenomena.

One must give prior consent before their inner band member may place them in a state of deep trance, for they have free will and cannot be controlled against their will. God the Great Spirit forbids those in the spiritual dimension from using anyone without their permission.

A trance medium that is placed in a semi-trance by his inner band member may feel as if their body experiences heaviness. They may be aware of their mouth opening and words being spoken yet are aware they have no control over what their inner band member is saying to those present.

When placed in a deep or complete trance, they are not aware of anything taking place around them. They will feel as if they are sleeping or in a state of total relaxation, and when their inner band member is finished the Trance Medium will awaken without any problems. They will not be aware of anything that was said by their inner band member or anyone who was present.

DARE TO THINK DEEPER, FOR HUMANKIND HAS THIS ABILITY AND NEEDS TO PUT IT TO GREATER USE.

CHAPTER FIVE: MENTAL MEDIUMSHIP

All that live in a human form in the physical dimension have in some degree the natural ability to develop their mental faculties over time and with the proper instruction some form of mediumship. In mental mediumship a spirit being from the spiritual dimension, such as a guardian angel, lowers their vibration in order to connect to the medium's vibration. The developing medium in turn works with his inner band in order to raise his vibration to meet theirs. Once their vibrations have connected the spirit being can then transfer their thoughts or images to the conscious mind of the medium using telepathic transference.

The medium (not a psychic) will receive the telepathic thoughts mainly through either clairvoyance (sight) or clairaudience (hearing) depending on that level of development they have attained. There are other aspects of mental mediumship but these two are the main focus for most individuals in the physical dimension.

Problems arise when the medium is poorly developed and they allow too much of their own personal influence or bias to cloud the spirit message they are trying to communicate to those in the physical dimension. The spirit entity may be sending a pure thought to the medium, yet the poorly developed medium may not be receiving it properly and/or in its completed form. Thus the medium is passing on information that may be distorted or so vague as to be useless to those seeking answers to their questions.

Do not be afraid to seek out mediums who give quality information, those who confuse, mislead or ask that you return for more info week after week seek only to line their pockets with your money. There are many that would take advantage, which casts a bad light on those mediums who truly care to be of service to humankind.

At this point let us discuss some of the better-known abilities dealing with mental mediumship. The main two are Clairvoyance and Clairaudience. Many people have experienced one or both of these on a limited basis in their normal lives. Some believe what took place, while others disregard what they saw or heard for fear of being labeled insane or a crackpot.

Clairvoyance or that which some call 'clear seeing' is what most individuals experience when they visit a medium for a session or reading as some refer to it. At no time does the medium see that which comes from the spirit dimension with their physical eyes. Everything that comes through is perceived mentally by the medium.

Clairvoyance has three main areas it can manifest itself through, which usually depend on the medium's mental, emotional, physical health, and the level of development they have reached as to what they can bring forth.

Some mediums have only one aspect of clairvoyance they can express while others may be able to express all or a combination thereof.

The first aspect of clairvoyance which the majority of medium's display to the public deals with one or more of the mediums inner band depositing their thoughts upon the mind of the medium. These thoughts can be conveyed through the use of simple concepts all the way up to using a hypnotic state or deep trance. This is done in one of three ways using symbols, vision, impressions or a combination thereupon.

The second aspect of clairvoyance in its main form is that of the medium being able to go beyond their physical sight to see through nontransparent matter. An example of this would be describing a certain person or location many miles away and what is taking place at that moment with that individual or that locality.

The third aspect of clairvoyance is termed impersonal or objective clairvoyance, which deals with the medium being able to view spirit beings and things in their environment in the spiritual dimension.

Clairaudience or 'clear hearing' is closely associated with clairvoyance in that most mediums who not only 'see' into another dimension, but can also 'hear' that which emanates from the other dimension.

In clairaudience the auditory message the medium receives comes to them as an actual voice they hear inside their head. Some mediums can tell which of their inner band members is speaking to them just by which ear they perceive to hear them with. As an example when a guardian angel speaks to his assigned medium it may always seem to that particular individual that his angel is speaking to his left ear. The chemist for that medium may give the impression of speaking to the right ear of the medium.

Just remember that mediums who rise up spiritually above the egotistical and self-seeking motives of the physical dimension are the ones who offer us the very best in spirit communication.

As an added note, only mental mediumship can be produced in the light, unlike physical mediumship, which can only be produced in near total darkness.

Let us talk for a moment on Trance and how it relates to mental mediumship. A spirit being from the spirit dimension works with a medium that has developed their mental abilities to such a point, that they can blend their vibrations and come into total harmony with the physical functions of the brain and body of the medium. Thereby sending their full expression of thought through the mental psyche of the medium, controlling the mediums speech patterns to where the spirit being can communicate with those in the physical dimension more directly. The medium's spirit inside the physical body does not leave during the time the inner band member is overshadowing their thoughts. This is because the spirit of the inner band member never enters the medium's physical body.

Trance contains seven degrees or levels of unconsciousness. From a light trance where the medium expresses their thoughts freely all the way to a deep trance where the medium is not conscious of what is being said or taking place around them.

MASTER THYSELF AND YOU MASTER THE WORLD.

MASTER THE WORLD AND YOU MASTER THE UNIVERSE.

MASTER THE UNIVERSE AND YOU BECOME ONE WITH GOD THE GREAT SPIRIT.

CHAPTER SIX: PHYSICAL MEDIUMSHIP

Physical Mediumship is where a spirit entity from the spiritual dimension uses a developed mediums power or energy to produce the desired effects, which can be viewed and heard by those seeking this type of communication or phenomena.

Such phenomena include Trumpet Speaking or what some call Direct Voice, Materialization, Spirit Photography, Automatic Writing, Apport Production, and Levitation just to name a few.

Ectoplasm is the material used by those in the spiritual dimension to produce or materialize themselves or objects in our physical dimension. A developed medium's body is where the ectoplasm is created and then used by those in the spirit dimension to manifest the desired phenomena. No special diet is needed for the medium to produce ectoplasm, their Chemist or Spirit Doctor simply balance and align the chemicals already found in their physical body in order to produce ectoplasm.

Ectoplasm is very sensitive to intense or bright light; thus most trumpet seances are conducted in darkened rooms, sometimes in dim red light. Ectoplasm can be brought forth in many forms; visible to the human eye or invisible, it may also be made to appear in any of the primary colors visible to humankind.

Mediums that have developed physical mediumship need to remain calm and have great self-discipline, for there is a need to avoid having anger control issues. Having an outburst of anger causes an imbalance in the chemical structure of the medium and thus affects their ability to produce ectoplasm.

Thoughts also have an effect on the physical body, which is why there are so few physical mediums of today who have developed their abilities to their fullest degree. Their Chemist or Spirit Doctor has difficulty maintaining the proper chemical balance when the medium changes their thoughts too often, such as excessive worry over events they have no control over. An example would be, if a plane crashes in another country and many are killed, that event should not cause great concern or worry on the medium's mind. Those that died chose the time and place of their exiting of the physical dimension in order to return to the spiritual dimension. Not everyone needs a full lifetime to attain what he or she came to learn or experience for their personal growth. Some only need short or limited times in this dimension to get the results they require. So don't worry and fret over great disasters that you cannot control, nor have any sway over.

Just know that in mental mediumship the conscious mind plays the major role, and in physical mediumship the unconscious mind plays the major role.

Let us discuss some of the different types or forms of physical mediumship starting with Trumpet or Direct Voice speaking. An aluminum trumpet is used mainly in voice seances because the spirit being wishing to communicate can easily manipulate the lightweight aluminum and can use the trumpet to manifest or materialize vocal organs within the trumpet in order to communicate with those present. This is made possible by the production of ectoplasm, which is drawn from the medium in order to materialize the vocal organs in the trumpet and also to levitate the lightweight aluminum trumpet.

The guardian angel or who ever is wishing to speak takes thought vibrations and converts them into sound vibrations in order to produce a distinguishable utterance for those present to hear clearly and loudly what information is to be given. At no time is the real voice of the physical medium used.

Materialization of a spirit being can be a partial materialization in which only a face or just a hand will be visible to those in attendance, or it can be a full and complete form that is materialized.

To begin with one needs a large room, many times a basement in a house, so that those attending the séance, basically nine to twelve individuals can fit comfortably therein. The medium is placed in a chamber, which is usually a set of black curtains that enclose the medium in order for the ectoplasm to be produced and used by the spirit being that desires to materialize.

The chamber is completely dark, yet the rest of the room is placed in red light or in semi-darkness in order for those present to view the phenomena being produced by the spirit. Regular light cannot be used due to the destructive nature of light on ectoplasm. Ectoplasm emanates from the left side of the entranced mediums physical body and the chamber the medium is contained in helps to protect the ectoplasm while the spirit uses it to bathe itself in the sticky substance in order to produce the desired materialization.

After the spirit has utilized the ectoplasm to cover its desired form, the spirit being then emerges from the chamber to be viewed and to communicate with those present in the semi-dark room. The spirit lowers its vibration level in order to be able to materialize and be observed by those in the physical dimension who are themselves vibrating at a lower level.

Depending on the level of materialization achieved, those in attendance may be allowed to touch the materialized spirit form, but only if told to do so by the materialized spirit, otherwise harm may be caused to the medium if the spirit does not have complete control of the ectoplasmic covering.

The spirit who is materializing concentrates his thought process in order to lower or slow down his vibrational level to where he is compatible to the physical dimension or denser matter he is trying to produce the phenomena in. Once this is achieved, the spirit can speak freely to those who are present and they in turn can seek answers to their personal questions.

Levitation involves the use of rods, made of ectoplasm, which are produced by those in the spirit dimension in order to lift objects in the physical dimension. These rods are usually not seen by those present but can be used under the right conditions to lift an individual up into the air or to lift objects into the air. An example would be that of lifting a chair containing an individual and moving the chair and individual from one room to another then back again.

KNOW THAT DEATH DOES NOT EXIST; ONLY CHANGE EXISTS, FOR YOU ARE CO-CREATORS WITH THE GREAT SPIRIT. JUST KNOW YOU WERE NEVER BORN AND YOU SHALL NEVER DIE, NO MATTER WHAT SHAPE OR FORM YOU TAKE IN OTHER DIMENSIONS INCLUDING THIS ONE.

CHAPTER SEVEN: DEVELOPMENT OF MEDIUMSHIP

This chapter is for those who may have an interest in developing one or more of those abilities spoken of earlier in this book. The ultimate purpose of all mediumship is to convey the message to those whose heart and mind are heavy in deep sorrow and confusion, that love is ever present and waiting to awaken them to the reason they incarnated into the physical dimension. To help guide them back onto their chosen path in this lifetime if they have lost their way in our chaotic world.

To begin with, there is a test assignment that is given for a sixty-day period to prove to your Guardian Angel that you are truly committed to developing some form of mediumship. Most individuals will not spend the necessary time required to develop their ability, thus the reason for the sixty-day test. Those who complete the test assignment will then be taken seriously by their Guardian Angel.

In our fast paced society of today, most individuals can't stay with something for six minutes before becoming bored and moving on to something new. Therefore sixty days may seem like an eternity to some and that should serve as a notice they are not ready for such an undertaking of this type, for it may take years to develop their ability.

The sixty-day test has two parts: First, right after going to bed, mentally call upon the positive forces in the spirit dimension to come join with you. Next, call for your Guardian Angel; ask that he place a protective shield around you straight from God, to keep you from any negative influence or negative thoughts as you sleep. Then ask your Guardian Angel to revitalize your physical body, to give it energy and power for the coming day.

An example would be, "Great Spirit, please allow the positive forces of the spirit dimension to join with me. This is (insert your first name) and I'm calling for my Guardian Angel. Please place a protective shield around me straight from God so no negative influence or negative thoughts can harm me. Please revitalize my body to give it energy and power for the coming day. Thank you."

Second, right after waking up in the morning, before getting out of bed, once again mentally call upon the positive forces of the spirit dimension to come and join with you. Call your Guardian Angel and ask that a protective shield be placed around you. Ask for guidance and help with any problems that may occur during the coming day.

An example would be, "Great Spirit, please allow the positive forces of the spirit dimension to join with me. This is (insert your first name) and I'm calling for my Guardian Angel. Please place a protective shield around me straight from God so no negative influence or negative thoughts can harm me. Please give me any guidance or help today with any problems that may arise during the day. Thank you."

Do this each morning and each night for the next sixty-days. If you stay with it and complete the test assignment, your Guardian Angel will then be willing to assist you with your development of Mediumship.

To begin this wonderful journey, meditation will form the foundation needed to develop your ability in mental mediumship. Here are the eleven steps to getting started:

1. Wear comfortable clothing that is loose fitting.
2. At first, it is best to use a straight-backed chair to sit in. Keeping the feet flat on the floor not crossed. Do not cross the arms, let the palms of your hands rest flat against the top of your thighs.

3. Sit in a quiet, semi-darkened room to begin with. The semi-dark will help you clear your mind of the day's worries. Later on when you are more at ease with your meditation you can start meditating in a more lighted atmosphere.
4. Say out loud this invocation, "Great Spirit, please allow the positive forces in the spirit dimension to come forth and join with me for this meditation class. I am seeking to develop my mental abilities in the way of mediumship. Please bring forth the white light that contains your love and wisdom, which we seek in earnest. I seal this humble prayer in faithfulness and in truth. So be it." Note: saying this invocation out loud will allow your Guardian Angel to lock onto your voice vibration, in which he can use your energy to assist him in lowering his vibration to be closer to you in the physical dimension. He can lower his vibration without your help; it just makes it easier if you assist him.
5. Call your Guardian Angel out loud, invite him to come and join with you for this meditation class.
6. Breathe IN and OUT in a slow, deep manner, for a total of seven times. First breathe IN and hold it for a count of seven, then breathe OUT and hold for a count of seven. Do this procedure seven times to relax the body and mind. Breathe IN through the nose, and OUT through the mouth.
7. Close your eyes. If you have trouble clearing your mind, simply play some soft meditative music. Concentrate on the music and relax. Do not fall asleep.
8. Meditate for 20 to 30 minutes or more if you have the time. Start out slow, don't rush your development, it takes time to prepare your body and mind for mediumship. If you feel fidgety after awhile, simply break off the meditation. Your Guardian Angel has probably stopped working on you at that point. Don't feel as though you must be punctual for the length of time you meditate. The important punctuality is the starting time. As for example: if you decide to meditate on Monday, Wednesday and Friday at 4:30pm, then be ready at 4:30pm each time. If you pick random times, your Guardian Angel may not always come due to things he is working on for his own personal progression in the spirit dimension. So if you are punctual at the same days and times, he will then make the time to be with you to work on your development.
9. Just a suggestion, meditate one day a week to start for 30 to 45 minutes. Once you feel comfortable you can increase the days and/or time later on. Do what feels right for you. If your friend says he/she is meditating every day for two hours, fine, but don't you feel pressured to follow their lead. Do what feels right for you, ease into your development; this is not a contest.
10. Let your Guardian Angel do the rest. He will rework your physical body from the inside in order for you to receive vibrations from those in the spiritual dimension. It takes time to restructure a physical body so be patient. Some individuals can develop quicker then others for no two humans are alike. Later, others will join with you to form an inner band to help with your development.
11. When you finish your development class mentally say, "I'm going to close now, I wish to thank all those who came to be with me for this development class." You're now done.

Now then, later on in your development when you start to receive images (clairvoyance) and/or start to hear (clairaudience) from your Guardian Angel mentally tell him what you see or hear, so he will know how much you are receiving. It lets him know what areas need adjustment or fine-tuned.

As an example, he may show you an image of a red fire truck in your mind's eye or what is called the third eye yet you may only see the fire truck in black and white. Mentally say I just saw a fire truck and it was in black and white. That lets him know you are not receiving in color and he will then work on you to the point where you will at some future time be able not only to see the fire truck, but to see it in color as he meant for it to appear. You may be shown such things as numbers, a person's face, a symbol or a name. It may be flashed into your mind very rapidly. You may only see for example three numbers in a triangle in black and white. Your Guardian Angel may have flashed six numbers in the color yellow surrounded by a red triangle. When you tell him what you saw, he then knows how far you have advanced in your development. Some individuals may start receiving in a short time; others may take years to fully develop, so stay focused and be patient.

WARNING! Do not rush into development too fast, your mental and emotional state of mind may become too intensified. Things you normally could deal with could have you in tears. If you feel emotionally out of control --STOP! --and wait thirty to sixty days before meditating again. You are overwhelming yourself with the vibrations of those in the spirit dimension. Their vibrations spin at a higher rate and when they come in contact with you to work on your development yours speed up for a time, and some individuals get over loaded mentally and/or emotionally. Use patience and common sense.

You may experience some of the following things; if you feel like you are spinning around or floating upward, especially while in bed, do not be concerned. Your Guardian Angel will work on your chakra centers from time to time. Chakras spin and vibrate, the only way your physical brain can understand what is happening is to view it as if the bed is spinning around or that your body is floating up above the bed. Just know, you are not floating off the bed and the bed isn't spinning, your Guardian Angel is simply speeding up your Chakras, enlarging, enhancing and enriching those centers that had no life in them before.

It is not spooky, scary or frightening, just an adjustment your Guardian Angel will make from time to time for your spiritual growth.

Some individuals may experience memory loss when their Guardian Angel works on their crown chakra. During meditation some individuals have experienced pinpricks around the head area, or felt as if something was being pumped into their head. Simply procedures needed to correct imbalances in the body.

Some individuals report seeing waves of colors, such as purple and white in their mind's eye while meditating. These two colors deal with purification and change of basic form into that of a more highly spiritual form. Other colors may be seen depending on what is needed to bring your physical system into harmony for your development.

Depending on what phase of mediumship you go into, you may experience headaches and/or stomachaches of short duration caused by the chemicals and the procedures used by your Guardian Angel. Others may experience profound headaches when their Guardian Angel starts to expand their third eye. "Spirits of Camphor" found in most drug stores will help with the headache and Vanilla Ice Cream will help relieve the stomach problems. When using the Spirits of Camphor apply it to the forehead with a cotton ball being very careful not to get it in your eyes. Then place a cold damp washcloth over the forehead and lie down in a dark, cool room until the ache runs its course.

Just know some individuals never have headaches or stomach problems, it depends upon the individual person, each experience things differently, and no two are alike.

Once your Guardian Angel gets in harmony and has basic control of your development it will not matter if you sit in a straight backed chair. You may sit in a more comfortable chair or even lie upon a bed or couch to meditate, as long as you remain awake and don't fall asleep.

These are just a few things some, but not all, individuals may experience during their development of Mediumship.

Just a short word on morality and ethics, you will attract to yourself those in the spirit dimension which are close to your vibration. An example would be; if you steal or cheat others, if you abuse or use your intellect to take advantage of those who are weak or less fortunate then yourself. You will not attract to yourself higher spiritual beings from the spiritual dimension to guide and assist you in your quest for development of mediumship. You will attract those who, like yourself, wish only to use and abuse you for their own amusement. There are many fakes and charlatans who feed off the misfortunes of others who seek help and guidance. In the end they cheat themselves out of their own spiritual progression.

Developing mediumship requires a great desire to help others in whatever way possible. If you seek only gain for yourself, then you will not benefit from your development, for it is meant to enlighten humankind to a higher understanding of God the Great Spirit.

Once you have been meditating for at least six months there is an exercise you may wish to try:
a. While meditating, in your mind visualize a tall majestic mountain.
b. Place a small room on top of this mountain. Visualize yourself building this room.
c. Inside this room, place the style and color of the furniture you wish to be there.
d. Over in one corner, visualize a curtain hanging there.
e. After you have completed your room, see yourself go over to the curtain in the corner.
f. Open the curtain and step through. See what happens next…?

Those who are trying to develop some type of Physical Mediumship; such as Materialization or Trumpet (also called Direct Voice) mediumship, can follow the same meditation routine as listed for Mental Mediumship. With the exception of #3, physical mediumship needs to be developed in a darkened room due to the disruptive nature of light rays upon ectoplasm, especially for any kind of materialization.

If at all possible, seek out a qualified teacher to guide you through your development. There are many spiritual camps and associations, which offer help and guidance for beginners. Be leery of those who ask for great sums of money for this assistance, true mediums desire to help others in order to advance their soul, not to fatten their bank accounts. Give freely to those who truly seek to know God the Great Spirit.

OUR BODIES NEED GOOD NUTRITION, PROPER REST AND BASIC EXERCISE TO FUNCTION IN OUR PHYSICAL DIMENSION.

OUR MINDS NEED KNOWLEDGE IN WHICH WE ARE RESPONSIBLE FOR TURNING THAT KNOWLEDGE INTO WISDOM, WHICH IS TO BE SHARED FREELY WITH ALL HUMANKIND.

CHAPTER EIGHT: TRANCE AND TRUMPET SÉANCE

The basis for a séance is simply for those in the physical dimension to communicate with those in the spiritual dimension.

The typical séance is conducted in a darkened room containing individuals who sit in a circle. The circle contains a trance medium who acts as the conduit to allow those in the spiritual dimension to speak through the trance medium with those individuals in the physical dimension seeking to speak with their loved one's who have returned home.

In a trance séance the guardian angel speaks through the trance medium, using his developed vocal cords. In a trumpet séance the guardian angel reproduces the vocal cords inside the trumpet itself in order to communicate, and the medium's body or vocal cords are not used for the communication. Just know a fully materialized spirit entity uses their own form or vocal cords to communicate and does not use the vocal cords of the medium.

Those individuals using a trumpet need to begin by washing their trumpet with warm water and mild soap in order to magnetize the aluminum cylinder. No one else is to touch or handle your trumpet. The first development class where you begin to use your trumpet simply hold the trumpet in your lap so that it can become attuned to your vibrational level and that of your inner band members who will be producing phenomena through it.

The following transcript is an actual tape-recorded séance of a trance medium giving a group of individuals the option of a Past Life Reading or a Future Life Reading. The names of those in attendance have been changed to protect their privacy and identities.

Dr. Woods: Yes, this is Dr. Charles Woods. I'm the guardian angel of this instrument. Greetings, my understanding is that some may be interested in past lives? I have looked into some past lives of this group present here tonight.
Now at this time I wish to give you a choice, and I want you to simply see before you two doors. The door on the left will be the door to a past life. The door on your right will be the door that opens to your next physical existence in the physical dimension. I will give you your choice of choosing whether you wish to have discussed a past life or the life that you will live next time you incarnate in the physical body of a human. This will be your choice, you see.
Now did everyone understand what I said?

Group: Yes.

Dr. Woods: All right then, Clark, do you want to go first?

Clark: Yes.

Dr. Woods: Which door do you choose, Clark?

Clark: The right door.

Dr. Woods: Now, I want you to understand that there is a law that I will be working under, and I'll explain it to you.

The law is that I will not give you a date, and I want to explain that. If I were to say, as an example: In the year 2121 you're going to be born and do this and that. Then when you reach a certain age in this life, you may say, "Hey, I've got to die in order to get over there in time to get everything ready for the next life."

You see? So I don't want that. So I will not give you dates. I wish it not to be in your subconscious mind.

Everyone understands that if you pick the door to your right, I will withhold the date because your subconscious mind will cause you concern and worry and a lot of wasted effort in thought.

However, I will tell you that, being in your subconscious, any information that is given to you while in the physical state will be most difficult to erase after you have been reincarnated. Do you understand?

You will have more recall than at the actual time of birth. The Spirit itself is being instructed into its earth life before birth. Do you understand?

Clark: No

Blanche: If you're born again Clark, you will remember what he's telling you now.

Dr. Woods: Because you are being given the information now, while you are in the human form, you will recall it in the next life. You will have more recall; you will remember what takes place here tonight. Understand?

Clark: Yes.

Dr. Woods: When you're living that future life, if I say on a particular day a certain thing will happen, you will have total recall and say, "Well I was looking forward to it happening."

Clark: I understand now.

Dr. Woods: Good, very well. Of course, for those who choose the door on the left, the recall will not have a plus or minus for you.

Sharon: I have a question, if you choose the door on the left, are they going to give dates?

Dr. Woods: Yes, dates are always given in past life readings.

Sharon: Oh, okay, I didn't know.

Dr. Woods: This knowledge will be coming from the Akashic Records. It might be called the Higher Hall of Records. It has many names or it means many different things to many different people. It is the Higher Hall of Akashic Records when the future life is there.

Now, I will begin with you Clark. If you have a question feel free at any time to ask. This is Dr. Charles Woods; I will be working tonight.

Clark: Okay.

Dr. Woods: In the future life, the life that is already planned, the life that has been laid out, the life that you are working towards now, that you are obtaining knowledge and information and being guided towards. I will now begin. I will turn the page of the book and I will start with the very beginning of the time of birth.

This may seem insignificant to you tonight but in the next life it will mean a great deal. It will mean a great deal to people who study the stars and the planets. So the time will be important to them and to you.

You'll be born the Earth time of 6:03am. It will be a Thursday. Your mother will end her physical existence at 6:08am, Thursday.

You will be raised in a home that is not unlike the homes of today of an orphanage, but it will be called more of a training institution.

Your father will not reject you, if you're wondering why the institution, your father will not reject you but it will be the way of the time that you have been born in.

Your father will be a man in the service of the government in the way of, not a politician, but as a keeper of peace. You may in your lifetime, this lifetime that you are living in now call the gentleman a career soldier. But he will be a gentleman of peace instead of this other term.

I will reveal to you at this time the names of those people. Your name will be…now this is no pun. Your name will be exactly the same as your first now, but it will be spelled backwards: Kralc. Do you understand?

Clark: Yes.

Dr. Woods: Very good. Your mother, whom you will never know, will be named Navarone. Your father's name will be Harmzes. The last name, the family name of your family will be Eiruman.

Now then, through the institutional care and through the studies and the schooling, you will go into the scientific study of planetary study. This will be a normal study for that time.

You will spend your career not upon this planet. Your life basically will be a dweller of space. You will be traveling from one area to another. Much similar to the airlines of today, which go from one city to another city or from one continent to another continent. But this will be of a more colorful, advanced type of flight.

You will never marry. You will perish and return to the spiritual dimension after a period of earth years numbering forty-seven. I will not disclose the nature of the death, for it will have no bearing upon this life when you do recall. You will be in another dimension. You will be in another galaxy, and you will perish. But know that you shall be as close to spirit then as you are now. There will be no reason to fear being lost there in a vast nothingness, because it is not a vast nothingness.

Clark: Will I have the same feelings and emotions as I have now?

Dr. Woods: No. You're going to be developed as a scientist. You will have no emotion. You will have feeling. You will not have emotions; you have primitive emotions now. You will not have emotions in this future life.

This is Dr. Charles Woods.

Clark: Thank you.

Dr. Woods: Now Blanche, are you ready? What door do you want?

Blanche: The left.

Dr. Woods: You wish to seek a past life experience. Very well, I'd like to place you at this time in the nation or country that is called Canada. I'm placing you there and giving you the name in which you will not enjoy. You have never in any life had a name you enjoyed. I wish to give you the name of your last, next to last incarnation. This is not the last one. This is the one before. The name that I give you is Bella.

Blanche: It's better than the one I got now.

Dr. Woods: Yes, but you didn't think so then.

Blanche: Probably not, its not the world's prettiest.

Dr. Woods: Now Blanche, like the "B" is very important in your life to you. You feel closeness to the "B" and I think it's because of the spirit God sound of "ob."

Now then, let us go along with this and you can see some of the character peculiarities coming out, because of that Canadian life and to this one. I skipped a life. It didn't show up in your last life that's the reason I picked the one before to speak on this evening.

This is why you are always hot. You like cool weather. You're cool natured. You like cool places. Many of your lives which have been few have been spent in cool areas on the Earth.

Now, the family name of this one of which I'm speaking of was Sheller. You were not French. You were a Duke's mixture. You were English. Your parents came from England.

Now, Bella Sheller was born in the year 1637. You were married and raised three children. You gave birth to seven children four did not live. They had short life spans. Three that survived lived to adulthood.

You were alone a lot in your life, for your husband was an explorer type. He was working for the government, so to speak, in bringing about mapping of the land. He was exploring the land areas for the leaders and officials of that time period.

You live to be the age of eighty-seven. So you may add your birth date to see the date you died, passed away. You passed away in October of that year, the 21st. The month of birth wasn't as important as it would have been to Clark. It was May 12th.

You had a great deal in common through that experience with the Indians in that area. You were not an Indian lover, but you tolerated the Indian people. You were no missionary by any means.

Blanche: What was my married name?

Dr. Woods: Bella Bonyea. He was French.

Blanche: Well, between this last life and the one in 1600 must have been a long time in between there.

Dr. Woods: Yes, you needed a long period of development in the spiritual dimension. Now then, do you have another question about that period?

Blanche: Is that the reason I want to go to Canada, because of that prior life?

Dr. Woods: Yes.

Blanche: Where did I live?

Dr. Woods: You were close to a large Indian village, or encampment they called it. This is Dr. Charles Woods.

Blanche: Oh, thank you.

Dr. Woods: Now then, let's see, Mike are you ready?

Mike: I'd like the door to the future.

Dr. Woods: I would like to explain how it is arrived at of a future existence. And it is the future life as programmed, so-to-speak, from your past experience. In many past lives you're being guided in a direction to be of future service in a coming life or experience. It is basically the same life; you are the same being, same person. You are being placed in a different experience.
Now Mike, are you ready to open the door on your right?

Mike: Yes.

Dr. Woods: Very well, again I will not give you dates or ages or years so as not to concern you dearly or deeply now.
In your next Earth experience you will be female. You will be from a large family.
The time and day of your birth I will give although it will not carry the importance to you that Clark's will to him. Your birth will be 8:12pm, on a Sunday. It will be raining.
As I spoke earlier, you will be of the female sex. You will have tremendous abilities as a child in the arts.
You will not marry young, but you will marry; however you will not produce children.

You will develop in your thirties a writing ability. You will write many volumes of knowledge on the arts. You will develop a philosophy through your writings.

You will, for a time, live in seclusion during your periods of deep thought in your career.

In your twilight years of your life you will expand and broaden out in the field of appearing before audiences in speaking and lecturing.

Your passing will be normal. Everything goes according to the records as I see them, you should live to be eighty-one years old in your next Earth existence. Not this one.

Now then, the birth name of this child will be a strange name too. It will be Feon Monet Break. When she does marry, the married name of the gentleman she marries will be Marchant. Okay?

Mike: Yes.

Dr. Woods: Now Judy, I have for you two doors, one on the left and one on the right. Which will be your pleasure?

Judy: Left.

Dr. Woods: We open the door and enter into a room of a past life. In the past life that you have completed, you are seeking some verification. I will give you something here for you to puzzle over. You were not a doctor; you were one who worked as a doctor.

I am placing you right in the middle of the Revolutionary War in this country. You were not Martha Washington, yet you knew of her and some others. But your name, a common name, was JoAnn Wilcox.

Now there were three marriages. JoAnn Wilcox Circee was the first, JoAnn Wilcox Circee LaMarz was the second and third was JoAnn Wilcox Circee LaMarz Blankenheimer, and it was a Jewish name. Two of the gentlemen were killed in the war and the other one outlived you. Yes, you lost two close together.

You were close to much of the fighting at that time, which spread all over a great area. Most of your life though was spent in the Virginia region.

Now then, May 30th was the date of your birth. The year was 1741. In Earth years you were going into your ninety-third birthday when you passed.

You were born in what the Indians called a wigwam.

Judy: I wasn't American?

Dr. Woods: Yes, you were an American citizen.

Judy: You said I wasn't a doctor?

Dr. Woods: You had a very limited nurse training, but you were called upon to do the acts that a doctor would do in a type of emergency. You did many midwife acts and you doctored many people. There were no doctors available many of the times in the areas where you were at, and you assumed the duties. You had a lot of courage. You had a lot of instinctive doctoring skill. You liked to use, or were adept at using a knife in the way of surgery.

Judy: Was this from a prior life?

Dr. Woods: Yes, I feel as though you got your fill.

Judy: I used up all my courage.

Dr. Woods: I will say this, in a prior life even before this one we're speaking of, you were a man. You were a brute. You did commit chaos and murder. You bludgeoned people to death with instruments of war.
 So in that life I am speaking of, the last one, the sight of blood and gore didn't annoy you.
 Now you have come a long way because you have outgrown that. See the improvements and progressions you've made?

Judy: Yes.

Dr. Woods: All right Sharon, which door would you like to choose?

Sharon: I'll go for the left one.

Dr. Woods: In your past life, I'm going to skip with you and at a later date I'll go into your last existence.
 I want to go back into time, when you were what many people of today would call a monk. You were of the male sex. You spent a great deal of time in monastery work, which was primarily praying, gardening and teaching.
 You had reached a certain knowledge and degree of your own. You did not pass away due to old age. When the hoards of Genghis Khan came through your area, you were cut down, decapitated. You lost your head, yours arms, your legs and were disemboweled. She may recall these pains at birth sometimes.
 Upon entering the monastery he did not take the vow of silence because he was a teacher and instructor.
 The name of the monk of this existence, because he was born to a family of prestige in that era, will not be given. I'll give him another name that is as close as the sound would be to us, a name that would be recognizable, Xavier. But it was of a different pronunciation. He went only by Xavier during that existence.
 Now the dates of passing, due to a new experience of another life that is to come, I wish not to divulge the date of death because of the horror of the death. The second of that death will carry over and into another life with a similar Earth experience. I wish not to place the date of death because the date will correspond with the coming date of death.
 That being the one that is important in mathematics in that lifetime, in that mathematical equation of death, she will find the answer. And it will cause much disturbance to her, so I will not divulge that date for her.
 Now, it is time to close. God Bless you all. This is Dr. Charles Woods.

WHAT APPEARS TO BE IS BUT AN ILLUSION. SEEK THE GOLDEN RING OF TRUTH, YOU SHALL FIND THE DESIRED DIRECTION IN LIFE.

CHAPTER NINE: AURA AND CHAKRAS

The human Aura radiates around the physical body in varied degrees of energy and colors, which correspond to the individual's current emotional, physical, mental and spiritual awareness at the time of viewing. Those from the spiritual dimension, such as your

Guardian Angel, and some developed mediums can perceive your aura and tell what is happening physically with you while you are in the physical dimension.

Auras are represented by colors to those who can perceive them. White conveys a blending of all colors whereas Black conveys the void or absence of color; this is why these two colors are mainly indeterminate or neutral from the others.

Red, Blue and Yellow form the main colors of an individual aura, with the other colors representing lesser energy layers.

Red is mainly an indicator of the physical state of an individual's mental activity while in the physical dimension. On the high end of the scale it concerns itself with purist thoughts concerning Love on all its grand levels and on the lower levels it deals with the basic emotions of anger and lust.

Yellow is mainly an indicator of the intellectual level of an individual's mental activity. It covers from the highest to the lowest levels of wisdom, judgement, inspiration, reasoning, analyzing and all the areas of logical operations.

Blue is the main level dealing with an individual's mental activity as pertaining to ones spiritual development. It concerns itself with the high ideals of love and admiration for ones spiritual development, or lack thereof.

These and all other color combinations form a picture of an individuals health as pertaining to the physical, mental, emotional and spiritual levels of one who lives in the physical dimension. Be aware that all living things contain an aura of varying degrees.

Chakras are contained within the colored levels of your aura. Chakras vibrate and spin. There are seven Chakra centers associated with an individual's framework.

The Crown Chakra is found at the top of the head area and harmonizes with the pineal gland, which is in control of the brain and nervous system.

The Brow Chakra is found in the middle of the forehead where the 'third eye' is noted to be. It harmonizes with the pituitary gland, which is in control of the forehead region, temples and carotid system.

The Throat Chakra is found at the base of the throat area, which harmonizes with the thyroid gland, which controls the throat, neck and brachial systems.

The Heart Chakra is found in the center of the chest area. It harmonizes with the thymus gland, which is in control of the heart, lungs, and both the cardiac and circulatory systems.

The Solar Plexus Chakra is found between the breastbone and the belly button. It harmonizes with the pancreas. It controls the intestines, stomach, eyes, liver, skin area and the muscular system.

The Spleen Chakra is found in the abdomen and it harmonizes with the gonads. It controls the reproductive system.

The Root Chakra is found between the sex organs and the anus area. It harmonizes with the adrenal glands, which control the skeletal framework; including the legs, feet, ankles and teeth. It also controls the spinal cord, bladder and lymph system.

IF EVERYONE ON EARTH SHARED SOME OF THEIR LOVE WITH A STRANGER, PEACE ON EARTH WOULD BE MORE THAN A POSSIBILITY; IT WOULD BECOME A REALITY.

CHAPTER TEN: POWER OF HEALING ABILITIES

There are two basic methods used in healing. Everyone on Earth has a spirit companion, such as their guardian angel; to assist them with fulfilling their individual life plan or blueprint while in the physical dimension.

The first healing method is called 'hands-on' healing. That is where you first call upon your guardian angel mentally. Ask him to place a shield of protection around you straight from God the Great Spirit.

Second, place your hands upon the individual whom you desire to receive the healing energy. With the individual sitting in a chair, stand behind them and place your hands one on each side of their head or place your hands one on each shoulder if possible, then close your eyes. If they are in a bed, place one hand on their forehead and one over the heart area. Mentally ask your guardian angel to send the healing energy from the spirit dimension, through you, down your arms into the individual or loved one in need of this healing energy. Visualize the individual in your mind walking through a beautiful field of flowers, smiling and in good health.

Just know you are not to send this healing energy yourself, your guardian angel or spirit companion is to do it, to keep you from getting ill yourself. Part of the energy used by your guardian angel will come from your physical body. Without shielding yourself, that energy would return to you and could bring illness with it. Don't weaken yourself.

When performing 'hands-on' healing, remain in contact with the individual for five to fifteen minutes and then remove your hands. In this application the healing energy is coming directly from the spiritual dimension to that of the individual's body in the physical dimension. This may be done several times a day or only once a day depending upon the nature of the illness or disease you are seeking the healing for.

The second method is self-healing. It is accomplished by calling your guardian angel and asking him to place a shield of love, harmony and protection around you straight from God the Great Spirit. Then place your own hand(s) on the area of your body in need of healing.

If you are unable to reach the area, simply sit or lie down. Ask your guardian angel for healing mentally, and name the affected area or the illness you seek help with. Visualize your affected area or body becoming whole and healthy again.

Repeat this each day for as long as the healing is required. You will start to see results after thirty days, more or less, depending upon the nature of the healing desired. So don't give up too soon if you feel nothing is happening.

Most individuals need to learn the lesson of patience. Things take time in the physical dimension to correct and overcome. Also remember, after your body is brought back to a higher level of health, if you return to the negative patterns that caused the illness or disease in the first place, you will no doubt suffer the illness or disease again. You must change your lifestyle to that of the positive in order to experience good overall health. You must do it; your guardian angel cannot live your life for you.

Now if you are sick to the point you are going to die, and you still have work or lessons to accomplish in the physical dimension, then your guardian angel will intervene with healing energy to get you through the sickness so you can complete your life plan. That is if it concerns death.

If you have something minor like a cold or the flu, you are on your own unless you ask for healing. You have free will you can be as sick as you wish and your guardian angel will simply not interfere unless you ask for help. Yet, if it concerns death, then he will intervene whether you ask or not, to keep you alive so you can finish your lessons.

Now if it is your time to die, then there is nothing that will stop your death from occurring. For your guardian angel is the one your Master Teacher will send to bring you home, back to the spiritual dimension. Once the decision has been made that it is time for you to return, no power on Earth can stop your departure.

Let it be known, some individuals, not all, who have come into the physical dimension program certain illness or disabilities into their life plan in order to help them with their own personal growth pattern. Almost all major events an individual encounters in their life were programmed by that individual for their own personal growth in order to grow spiritually. There are no accidents in the physical dimension.

Prevention of disease is of far greater importance than curing disease after it has a hold on the individual. Proper diet and positive thinking are the two most important things in fighting illness and disease. The individuals mind controls the physical body, whereby positive or negative thoughts do affect whether we succumb to illness or disease, and also how well we can overcome disease that has already taken root in our physical systems. That's if it wasn't something you programmed into your life blueprint before you incarnated. Free will leads many down a destructive path of physical abuse against their own bodies. Such as poor eating habits, alcohol and/or drug misuse, and the like cause many in the physical form problems they did not seek to face in their life plan.

One of the law's of healing is to think positively on forgiving yourself and forgiving all others who have done you harm physically, mentally, emotionally and/or spiritually. Be earnest and totally honest in your forgiveness in order for it to have the proper effect. Health is the combination of mind, body and spirit, rather than seeing each as an individual component, all three need to be seen as a complete unit. You need to treat the whole individual, not just the symptom. Seek out the root cause in order to heal the total being.

Never use medicine made from experiments performed on animals. God the Great Spirit never intended for lower life forms to be used to cure humankind's afflictions. God has provided through the many herb-forms of nature and the healing energies of the spiritual dimension all that is necessary to cure the ills of humankind. Animals are placed in our protective care and to some extent it is our responsibility to see that they grow and prosper in their own growth patterns.

Now let us talk about specific things that humankind should be made aware of, such as the following:

Sudden Infant Death Syndrome – 'SIDS' or what is also called 'Crib Death' has a number of causes, I will simply provide at this time the most universal cause of Crib Death.

Let us for example take Spirit-X. Spirit-X planned his lifetime to where he would live to be seventy years old and then return to the spiritual dimension, or as some would say he died at age seventy.

So Spirit-X was incarnated into a human body and lived to be seventy. Let's say he died three months earlier than his full seventy-year period he planned on due to being over-medicated by his physician. He was in great pain, the Doctor gave him stronger medication and it stopped his heart three months before he was programmed to die.

Spirit-X in desiring to fulfill that human experience of seventy full and complete years —of which he was cheated out of three months—could be reborn into another incarnation and live three months as a newborn baby and then abort that life and return to the spirit dimension.

Then that would have satisfied Spirit-X's programmed seventy-year period to where he would feel as though he had achieved what he had set out to accomplish.

Another example of Crib Death would be a new spirit being born into a physical body and discovering that it has an illness or medical condition that it did not program for its personal growth. Something the parent had passed on to the infant's physical body which the new spirit had not foreseen. If the spirit feels that the disease or condition is too much for it to deal with, it simply leaves the body. Other spirits faced with the same decision may choose to remain in the unhealthy body and see its limitations as a challenge.

Some spirits who incarnate seek out certain parents it feels it will be in harmony with in order to achieve its main growth pattern. If the spirit is born, and then discovers the parents are no longer in harmony with each other; such as bickering and fighting over the cost and burden they now face in raising an infant. The spirit needing a harmonious set of parents in order to achieve its goals will abort that life in search of more loving and caring parents.

Just know the spirit has the ability to relieve itself of that experience, that life, where it simply leaves the body of the infant, abandons it. Without the spirit inside of it the physical body dies. A spirit has up to the approximate age of two to decide if it wishes to stay or leave the physical dimension.

Physicians then unable to find a medical cause term it to be a Crib Death. If no medical reason can be found for a baby dying, then it is due to the spirit leaving the body for its own personal reasons. It leaves not to punish the parents, but for its own personal reasons to fulfill its own personal blueprint or life plan.

Acquired Immune Deficiency Syndrome – 'AIDS' is kind of like when Adolf Hitler of Germany destroyed millions of Jews, it serves a dual purpose for the benefit of humankind. Not only does it teach a global lesson, it also teaches individual lessons for those living in the physical dimension and it helps Mother Nature de-populate the Earth.

If there were no diseases or disasters on Earth, humankind would not have the opportunity to reach out, to be more loving, more understanding toward each other in times of crisis.

When those in the spiritual dimension realized that humankind in the beginning only saw AIDS as a 'gay' disease, it was then decided for the benefit of all humankind to allow this disease to spread. Women, children and so-called 'straight' men become infected to gain the attention it was to have fostered in humankind to begin with. In order to force individuals to react and evolve in order to grow in the way of building character. God the Great Spirit loves <u>all</u> his children.

Teenage Suicide – Humankind already has many explanations concerning teenage suicide put forth by your psychiatrists and psychologists. Let us then add yet another cause to the list.

When a person dies, returns to the spiritual dimension, no matter at what age they may be at the time of their death, they will regress in appearance back to the time when they were most vibrant in the physical dimension.

For example if your most vibrant time was at age nineteen, and you attained the ripe old age of eighty-eight when you died. When you return to the spiritual dimension you will slowly regress in appearance back to how you looked at nineteen your most vibrant time in that life. Just know not everyone has their most vibrant time in their teens, some attain it in there thirties, forties, fifties and so on.

Suicide then, for some, but not all, teenagers happens when, during the emotionally and mentally confusing period of their youth, their subconscious mind may know that this is going to be their most vibrant time of life. In their confused state of mind they may think that this is the highest point they will ever achieve in life that they can go no higher.

They then commit suicide trying to comply with their subconscious thoughts that they have attained their goals in life and are ready to return to the spiritual dimension, even though their life plan called for them to live, for example, ninety-one years in the physical dimension.

For some, this is a lesson they are trying to overcome. The urge to commit suicide, life after life may be a pattern that if they master it and progress onward they will then satisfy that growth, that experience which they felt was needed in order to progress to the next level in the spiritual dimension.

Cancer – Many find this disease to be the major illness to fear when compared to most of the other illnesses humankind face.

There are many types of cancer and there will not be one cure that remedies them all. The many different cancers affecting humankind come from many different origins. A cancer in an individual may find its cause in the physical, mental, emotional or spiritual realms.

Treatment depends upon the reason you have developed a cancer. Everything from not taking care of your physical body--such as poor diet, no exercise--all the way to negative thinking, using drugs made from animals which were exposed to cruelty and the like, you have brought the cancer upon your spiritual self in order to learn the lesson of love.

Cancer can teach a great lesson for those who open up to it. There are those individuals who intentionally program cancer into their blueprint in order to force themselves to think deeper about what life and love really convey to us on a spiritual level.

Sitting in front of the cable TV or playing on the Internet day after day as our lives pass by is not enlightening in any way, shape or form. Cancer is but one of many diseases that pull us from our complacency and refocus us on the reason we incarnated in the first place, which is to advance our spiritual growth through the understanding of love.

MANY SEEK THE ETERNAL TRUTHS OF THE GREAT SPIRIT.

MANY SPIRITS IN THE PHYSICAL DIMENSION DO NOT KNOW WHO THEY ARE, WHY THEY WERE BORN INTO THIS DIMENSION, AND WHAT IT IS THEY MUST ACCOMPLISH BEFORE THEY RETURN TO THE SPIRITUAL DIMENSION.

IF YOU SUCCEED IN AWAKENING JUST ONE SPIRIT TO THE ETERNAL TRUTHS OF GOD THE GREAT SPIRIT, THEN YOUR EXISTENCE, YOUR LIFE ON EARTH HAS NOT BEEN WASTED.

CHAPTER ELEVEN: GOD'S LAWS

The natural laws or what some have termed the universal laws of God the Great Spirit are designed to regulate all that occurs within the scope of the created physical dimension. Nothing occurs outside these natural laws, for all individuals are governed and subject to their effects. Those who claim to have witnessed a miracle or some divine supernatural event simply do not understand the way God's laws work. For to understand the true application of natural laws one would not see miracles but see God's natural order working as it was meant to be.

Individuals and countries which work against these natural laws set forth by the Great Spirit bring chaos and great suffering upon themselves, which in turn can be alleviated by positive thinking and positive action. Working with God's laws and not against them can correct even the most negative transgressions committed by humankind.

Here are a few of God's natural laws governing the physical dimension, just note, there are many more but these will give you an idea of how things are governed in the physical dimension:

1. Law of Karma – Karma is a term which implies cause and effect. It is simply a philosophical term, do good and good will come to you, and do bad and bad will come to you in this life or the next. Just know this is NOT one of God's laws and it does not work as it is stated. Individuals bring upon themselves cause and effect for their own individual progression in the physical dimension. We create 'cause' by our very thoughts, good or bad, which set in motion the 'effect' that we must deal with in our life. Whether we bring forth-positive thoughts or negative thoughts-we are responsible for how our lives play out. If you are not happy, it's not someone else's fault, it is your own individual thoughts that have placed you on this path. Change begins with you.
2. Law of Grace – this is one of the Great Spirits laws and it truly works for those who believe and willingly accept it. Simply love yourself and all others in the physical dimension as you love God the Great Spirit.
3. Law of Relativity – all who are born in the physical dimension will be tested, this is done to build our individual character, for our spiritual progression. From the day you are born to the day you die you will receive tests.
4. Law of Attraction – simply stated, you attract those who are like yourself, if you are negative then negative will be attracted to you, if you be positive then positive will be drawn to you.

5. Law of Freedom – is basically free will given to each individual to follow their path or blueprint in life or to alter that path at anytime time and go down another path.
6. Law of Compensation – whatever you do comes back to you sooner or later. Do good and good will come forth. Do bad and bad will come to you.
7. Law of Love – God the Great Spirit is all unconditional love; therefore all love is God the Great Spirit, very simple indeed. The creative force of life itself is love.
8. Law of Truth – is the wisdom and knowledge of positive thinking.
9. Law of Oneness – all thoughts affect everything in the physical dimension, thoughts have force and interact upon everything else. Nothing goes untouched.
10. An unwritten law that is of God states that no one can overshadow or take control of your mental or physical abilities against your will. No one from the spiritual or physical dimensions can manipulate you without your consent.

THE HUMAN BODY IS THE HOME FOR YOUR SPIRIT WHILE YOU LIVE IN THE PHYSICAL DIMENSION.

THE SOUL OR ETHERIAL BODY IS THE HOME FOR YOUR SPIRIT WHILE YOU LIVE IN THE SPIRITUAL DIMENSION.

WHEN YOU PROGRESS OUT OF THE SPIRITUAL DIMENSION YOU ENTER THE TRUE DIMENSION WHERE NO SHAPE OR FORM IS NECESSARY. YOU ARE NOW TRUE SPIRIT.

YOU ARE STILL AN INDIVIDUAL ENTITY AND STILL FACE MANY NEW ADVENTURES, FOR YOUR PROGRESSION NEVER ENDS.

CHAPTER TWELVE: DECISION TIME or NDE

NDE or Near Death Experience is simply a time to decide if you are ready to leave the physical dimension or if you feel you need to stay for some important reason.

For those who don't know what NDE refers too, it simply tells of an individual's understanding of what happened. For example, after a devastating automobile wreck you were taken to the hospital. You were pronounced clinically dead and then revived, to the physician and all present in the operating room only a few minutes may have passed, whereas to the individual it may seem as if an hour or more has passed in which they were fully aware of what was taking place around them.

Nearly ten million American's have experienced an NDE, not to mention those whom for whatever reason have decided to keep their NDE to themselves. If you include the world millions have experienced a NDE whether reported or not.

The general experience by the average individual of a NDE consists of the following pattern:
1. The unanticipated comprehension that something dyer has happened and that the individual did not survive the event.
2. The feeling of leaving one's own body and floating several feet above it, while hearing and seeing everything taking place around their body.
3. Then an awareness of no longer feeling pain or stress, but an overwhelming sensation of being loved and feeling harmony and peace.
4. Many have an impression of being drawn toward a tunnel or gateway of some type.
5. While in the tunnel or near the end, individual's report seeing deceased family members, old friends or even some type of spiritual figure waiting to greet them.
6. After this reunion a being of beautiful light comes forth and shows them a review of the life they have led up to that point.
7. At that point some individuals are asked if they wish to return to the physical dimension in order to complete a lesson or some mission, or do they wish to stay in the spiritual dimension. Others are not asked, but simply returned whether they wish to stay or not, it is not their decision to make and are returned to their physical body.

Some might ask why those in the spiritual dimension allow such a thing as a near death experience to take place. Here is but a few reasons why we incarnate into this physical dimension:

a. To change an individual's view of the physical dimension in order to better understand the spiritual dimension.
b. To give them a better understanding and meaning of life in general.
c. To have no fear of death and to become more involved with taking care of Mother Earth.
d. Concern with personal growth in caring for oneself, empathy and compassion for the plight of others.
e. To attain spiritual growth and/or unconditional love as an individual entity.
f. To advance to higher levels and sub-levels in the spirit dimension.
g. For some it is a teaching mission to help those who seem lost in the chaos of the physical dimension.
h. To become closer to God the Great Spirit.
i. To study God's laws in order to see if the individual truly understands the operation of such laws.
j. To understand our place in God's overall plan, that we are co-creators within God's plan.
k. And many others.

EPILOGUE

This book is for those individuals who no longer need the misguided support of religion, but are ready to progress onward in their spiritual development.

Not everyone is ready to advance, and grounding themselves in some form of organized religion is fine. If the path you have chosen has led you to place yourself in the mists of a religious group, then so be it. For that may be where you are currently in your personal growth.

When you have sufficiently grasped the limitations of religion then you will no longer need its erroneous support and you will be ready to evolve to the next phase of your spiritual development.

Peace in the physical dimension may seem unattainable, but it is within humankind's destiny to focus on the true and positive affirmations that lead to World Peace. The wisdom to bring humanity to such a state already exists deep within our very souls, we just need to connect to it and bring it forth through the wonderful abilities God the Great Spirit has given us. Seek within, find your true path and connect to God.

Humankind will one day understand why their loving God has allowed them to experience; disease, murder, starvation, rape, war and the like…and they shall be so very thankful for those physical dimension lessons, and once we realize the true lessons, humankind can grow beyond the chaos of today's world.

It all begins with each individual, YOU!

CPSIA information can be obtained
at www.ICGtesting.com
Printed in the USA
LVHW062016131021
700250LV00017B/74